MW01714603

Burning Myself Alive

and other things better than talking to my ex.

First Printing: 2018

ISBN: 978-1-387-48273-3

My once-lover,

I'd love to never see your face again.

It would bring me all the joy in the world,
the kind of joy you can only find on models in
Christmas catalogues who have finally found
the perfect new all-in-one kitchen appliance.

In fact,
not talking to you is at the top of my Things To Do,

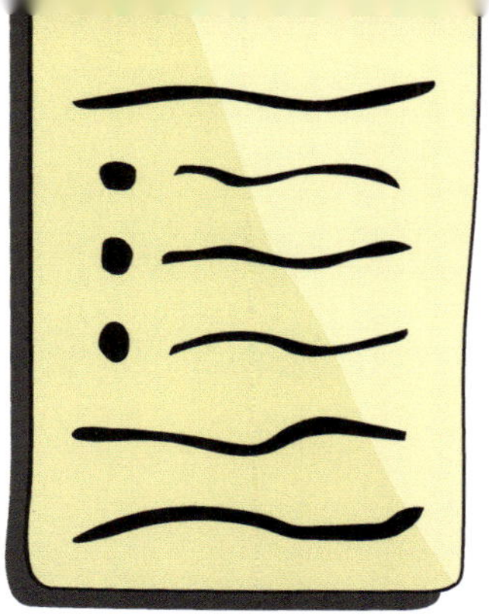

and talking to you is at the bottom,
right under a painful death,

like burning myself alive.

I would take sharks,

a whole tank-full,
all ripping me to pieces,

before I'd go out for a cup of coffee,
and 'just chat.'

And I would take a beehive for dinner,
oh, I'd eat the whole thing,

if swallowing live hornets meant not having
to use my oesophagus to produce sound
to make words that were in a
conversation between us.

It's like in that movie,

the one with all the cocaine,

where the guy is shot for like,
thirty seconds by machine guns,
and then the guy in sunglasses comes up
from behind and shoots him with a shotgun,
and he falls off the balcony and into the
indoor pool under that big neon sign
that says 'THE WORLD IS YOURS',

because I would rather take that,
than a single verbal interaction with you.

And sometimes when my phone buzzes,
my heart palpitates, because of primal
fear that you are the sender,

and I look around me,
and think of all the ways I could
avoid sending a message back.

Like once, at a restaurant,
when I imagined walking into the kitchen,
and putting both my hands in a food-grade blender
meant for cleverly-named smoothies,

so there could be no possible way
my fingers could text back.

Or once, at a concert,
when I quite literally weighed
my options and decided that yes,
climbing on stage and stabbing both
my eyes with the drummer's sticks,
then being tazed by security,

would be a walk in the park
compared to pulling out my phone,
and seeing your name.

God,
all the sharp objects I'd swallow,
and pass in agonizing bowel movements,

or the chemicals I would soak in,
that would corrode my skin,
and probably my skeleton too,
over saying a word to you.

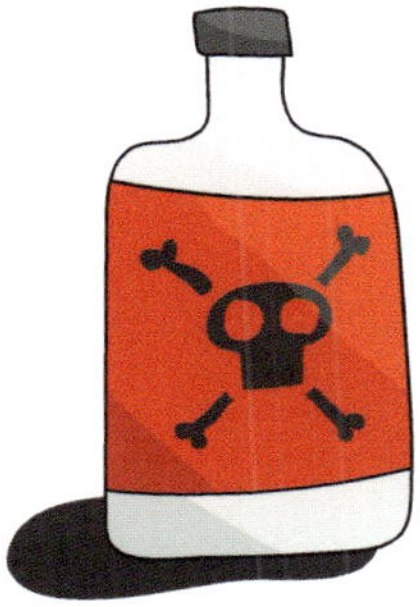

And if I ever saw your face, oh God,
like in a public park,
or a theatre lobby,

I think I would nearly die,

not because of your sight,
but because I would throw myself off a high object,
like the lobby balcony or a big tree,

and be rushed to the hospital in an ambulance,
to live the rest of my life in a vegetative state,
like that movie where the guy blinks a lot,
and hopefully be blind and deaf,
so as to not hear or see you.

My once-darling,

I wonder sometimes,
if you think about these things too,
and how far you'd go to not talk to me.

Because I guarantee I'd go further.

If you would jump from a skyscraper,
I would jump from a plane,
and rig the parachute without the instructor's knowledge,
and splat on the ground like a grape.

And if you would gouge out your eyes,
and cut your vocal cords,
I would put my neck under a whole damn mitre saw,
and pull the handle down really slowly,
so I really savoured it.

But I'm sure you don't think about it.
I'm sure you are happy in your new life.

Woohoo for you.
You always liked to rub it in.

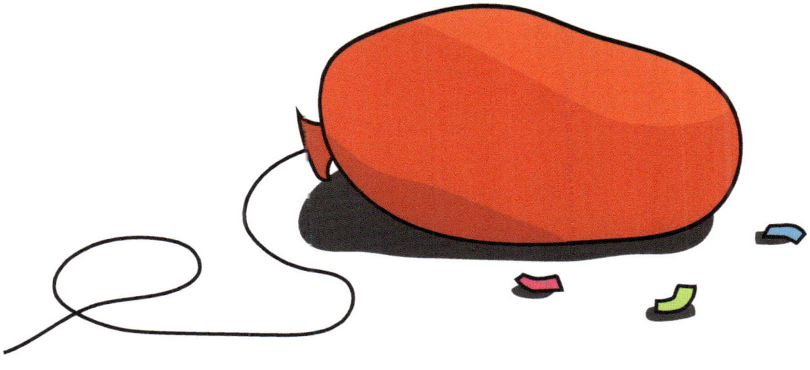

Well my once-friend,

even if you don't think about me at all,
or think about us talking,

I still wouldn’t do it.

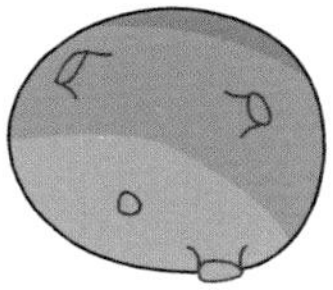

And I would kill myself to the moon and back before we did.

Because I'm still upset,

and I just wish you'd fucking know that.

CPSIA information can be obtained at www.ICGtesting.com
Printed in the USA
LVIW01n1256090218
565953LV00002B/3